SUPER SHEROES
OF SCIENCE

Investigating
Nature

Women Who Led the Way

ANITA DALAL

Children's Press®
An imprint of Scholastic Inc.

Library of Congress Cataloging-in-Publication Data

Names: Dalal, Anita, author.

Title: Investigating nature : women who led the way / by Anita Dalal.

Description: First edition. | New York, NY : Children's Press, an imprint of Scholastic Inc., 2022. | Series: Super SHEroes of Science | Includes bibliographical references and index. | Audience: Ages 8–10. | Audience: Grades 4–6. | Summary: "Summary: "This brand-new series highlights some of the major contributions women have made in the world of science. Photographs throughout"— Provided by publisher.

Identifiers: LCCN 2021037454 (print) | LCCN 2021037455 (ebook) | ISBN 9781338800470 (library binding) | ISBN 9781338800487 (paperback) | ISBN 9781338800494 (ebk)

Subjects: LCSH: Women scientists—Biography—Juvenile literature. | Women in science—Biography—Juvenile literature. | Women in science—History—Juvenile literature. | BISAC: JUVENILE NONFICTION / Biography & Autobiography / Women

Classification: LCC Q130 .D35 2022 (print) | LCC Q130 (ebook) | DDC 509.2/52—dc23

LC record available at https://lccn.loc.gov/2021037454

LC ebook record available at https://lccn.loc.gov/2021037455

Picture credits:

Photos ©: cover top: John Innes Archive Courtesy of the John Innes Foundation; cover center top: Picture Alliance/DPA/Bridgeman Images; cover center bottom: "Roger Arliner Young", 2012-06-11, https://hdl.handle.net/1912/16952; cover bottom: Science History Images/Alamy Images; 5 left: John Innes Archive Courtesy of the John Innes Foundation; 5 center left: Picture Alliance/DPA/Bridgeman Images; 5 center right: "Roger Arliner Young", 2012-06-11, https://hdl.handle.net/1912/16952; 5 right: Science History Images/Alamy Images; 6 inset top: John Innes Archive Courtesy of the John Innes Foundation; 7 bottom: Ruben Gutierrez/Dreamstime; 8 top: Picture Alliance/DPA/Bridgeman; 8 center: mauritius images GmbH/Alamy Images; 10 bottom: Prashanth Vishwanathan/Bloomberg/Getty Images; 11 top: Pallava Bagla/Corbis/Getty Images; 12 inset top: Alfred Eisenstaedt/The LIFE Picture Collection/Shutterstock; 17 top: Alexandros Michailidis/Alamy Images; 18 top left: Hank Walker/The LIFE Picture Collection/Shutterstock; 20 inset top: Avalon/Bruce Coleman Inc/Alamy Images; 21: Bettmann/Getty Images; 22 bottom: Steve Bloom Images/Alamy Images; 23 top: Penelope Breese/Liaison/Getty Images; 24 top: Konrad Wothe//imageBROKER/Alamy Images; 24 bottom: Fabian Plock/EyeEm/Getty Images; 25 top: Kirsty Wigglesworth/WPA Pool/Getty Images; 26 top left: United Archives GmbH/Alamy Images; 28 inset top: Kyodo News Stills/Getty Images; 32 center: Miguel Riopa/AFP/Getty Images; 35 top: Pictorial Press Ltd/Alamy Images; 36 bottom: "Roger Arliner Young", 2012-06-11, https://hdl.handle.net/1912/16952; 37 top: The Bancroft Library, University of California; 38 top: GL Archive/Alamy Images; 39 top: Nancy R. Schiff/Getty Images; 39 bottom: Connie Bransilver/Science Source; 40 top left: Phil Degginger/Alamy Images; 40 bottom left: American Philosophical Society/Science Source; 40 bottom center: JohnGaffen3/Stockimo/Alamy Images; 40 bottom right: Snap/Shutterstock; 41 top left: Ben Hider/National Geographic/Picture Group/Sipa USA/Newscom; 41 top right: Kimberly White/Breakthrough Prize/Getty Images; 41 bottom: Picture Alliance/DPA/Bridgeman Images; 42–43: pop_jop/Getty Images; 44 top: Avalon/Bruce Coleman Inc/Alamy Images; 44 center left: Science History Images/Alamy Images; 44 bottom: Kyodo News Stills/Getty Images; 45 top: Kyodo News Stills/Getty Images; 45 bottom left: John Innes Archive Courtesy of the John Innes Foundation.

All other photos © Shutterstock.

10 9 8 7 6 5 4 3 2 1   22 23 24 25 26

Printed in the U.S.A. 113
First edition, 2022
Series produced for Scholastic by Parcel Yard Press

Contents

Super SHEroes Change the World

Women scientists, engineers, and inventors have made remarkable breakthroughs for centuries. Often, however, their achievements went unrecognized. Today far more women work in these fields than ever before, and their achievements are celebrated.

This book celebrates the life and the work of thirteen of these women, thirteen Super SHEroes of Science!

The Super SHEroes of Science in this book all worked, or continue to work, to investigate nature.

Nature refers to things in the world, such as animals, plants, and the weather, that are not made by people.

SUPER SHEroes OF SCIENCE

Janaki Ammal

Jane Goodall

Roger Arliner Young

Rachel Carson

These Super SHEroes of Science changed the world in many different ways. They invented new ways to grow crops, studied the lives of chimpanzees, cared for marine animals, and warned of the terrible effects of harmful chemicals. And many of these women started off by being told that science wasn't for them. But they stuck to their dreams, asked questions, and took risks. They eventually got to write their own stories.

This book brings their stories to you! And while you read them, remember:

Your story can change the world, too! You can become a Super SHEro of Science.

Janaki Ammal

Janaki Ammal spent her life studying plants, especially those of her native country, India. She became famous for creating new types of crops. She also increased the world's knowledge of India's plants.

SUPER SHERO OF SCIENCE

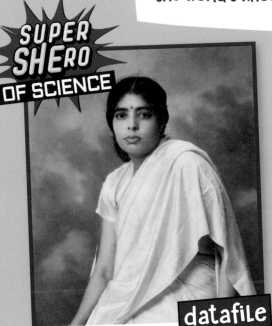

Janaki grew up surrounded by nature. Her family had a large garden at home. When she was in her teens, they encouraged Janaki to go to college, which was very unusual in India. At the time, most Indian women were not taught to read, so very few went to college. But Janaki got a degree in **botany**. She then won a scholarship to study in the United States. There she studied how plants can be used to create new types of plants.

datafile

Born: 1897

Died: 1984

Place of birth: India

Field: Botany

Super SHEro for: Teaching the world to understand the importance of India's biodiversity

Janaki used her knowledge to help her home country. People in India used a plant called sugarcane to manufacture sugar. However, Indian sugarcane contained less sugar than that from the Indonesian island of Java. For this reason, India imported sugarcane from Java.

Janaki bred sugarcane with other plants. Breeding means controlling the way plants reproduce so they produce more and better quality offspring. Janaki developed types of sugarcane that grew well in India and that also contained a lot of sugar. India no longer needed to import sugarcane.

Sugar from sugarcane is used to make candies, desserts, and drinks.

India has the second-largest sugarcane harvest in the world after Brazil.

What's Your Story?

Early in her career, Janaki traveled to the United States to continue her education. She believed that was the best way to learn more about botany. In 1931, she became the first woman from India to receive a PhD (the most advanced degree) in botany.

Have you ever been the first to receive anything? How did it make you feel?

The garden at Wisley

Despite Janaki's success, she faced **discrimination** because she was a woman and she came from a poorer family. In 1939, she moved to Britain, which at the time governed India.

While she was there, she and a colleague compiled a book listing the **chromosomes** of about 100,000 plants. The book showed which plants would breed together. It is still used to create new combinations of plants.

Janaki also became the first woman to work for the Royal Horticultural Society, Britain's main gardening organization. At the society's garden at Wisley, she experimented with getting plants to grow more quickly. Janaki bred a magnolia with white flowers. The Janaki magnolia was named in her honor.

In 1947, India became independent from Britain. Shortly after that, the prime minister of the new nation asked Janaki to help improve India's crops. In the early 1950s, Janaki became head of the main botanical **laboratory** in India.

Janaki's magnolias still grow at Wisley.

Did You Know?

Chromosomes are the structures inside the nucleus of a cell that control the individual characteristics of living things, such as plants and animals. They play a key role in passing qualities from parents to their offspring. The science that studies this process is called genetics.

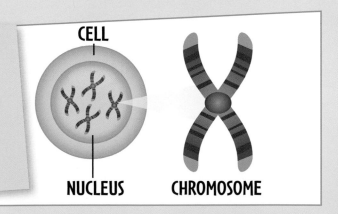

CELL

NUCLEUS   CHROMOSOME

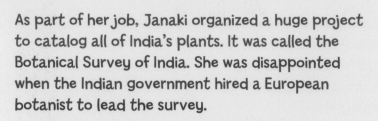

As part of her job, Janaki organized a huge project to catalog all of India's plants. It was called the Botanical Survey of India. She was disappointed when the Indian government hired a European botanist to lead the survey.

Janaki thought Indian botanists should study Indian plants. She believed that Indians had valuable knowledge about plants that had been gained over thousands of generations of people living in the region.

A mango orchard in India

Toward the end of her life, Janaki became concerned that too much vegetation in India was being cleared to create farmland. She campaigned to stop the government building a dam in the Silent Valley. This area had many special plants. Eventually the government abandoned the plan. The Silent Valley became a national park instead.

By then, Janaki had died at the age of eighty-seven. **She had made a valuable contribution to protecting biodiversity in India.**

Today, female botanists still play an important role in improving crops in India.

What Would You Do?

As you've read, Janaki wanted to help her fellow Indians but faced discrimination because she was a woman and because she came from a part of society that was disadvantaged.

Do you think that was fair?

If you were Janaki, how would you have reacted?

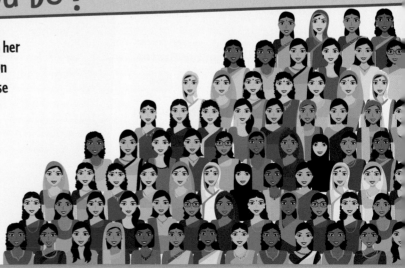

Rachel Carson

Rachel Carson was a scientist who studied how chemicals can affect the **environment**. She became famous for writing about nature and warning people about the dangers of chemicals that kill bugs.

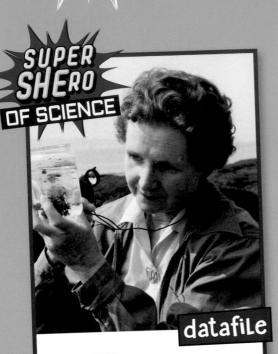

datafile

Born: 1907

Died: 1964

Place of birth: United States

Field: Biology

Super SHEro for: Protecting the environment by calling for harmful chemicals to be banned

Rachel lived in Pennsylvania. She studied **biology** in college and then went to work for the US Bureau of Fisheries, the government department in charge of the fishing industry. She studied creatures that live in the sea.

Rachel was asked to write articles about sea life by a magazine. Rachel was a great writer. She brought the undersea world alive. She described how, beneath the surface, the sea was full of life.

A tide pool by the sea

Rachel wrote more articles. She also wrote a book called *The Sea Around Us* to show readers how much humans depend on the oceans. It became a bestseller. Rachel was very shy, but she became a star.

She wrote two other books about the ocean. Readers loved them because they told fascinating stories and contained lots of information.

In her writings, Rachel explained that the oceans were very fragile. She warned that humans were damaging the ocean with pollution. Pollution includes harmful materials such as chemicals and waste that damage air, water, or soil.

A plane sprays crops with chemicals.

Rachel loved all of nature. She learned that farmers used a **pesticide** called DDT to kill bugs that ate their crops. Rachel spent five years researching DDT. She learned it also killed birds that ate the bugs. If it got into streams or rivers, it killed fish. Rachel wrote about DDT in her book *Silent Spring*. She said that, if the use of DDT continued, the birds could all be killed. The spring would be silent because there would be no birdsong.

What's Your Story?

Rachel was inspired by other women throughout her life. One was her biology teacher Mary Scott Skinker. Mary helped Rachel get her first job. The two women were lifelong friends.

Which women inspire you?   What do you admire about them?

Rachel explained how the death of birds would be a disaster for the environment. She said DDT could even poison people and make them very sick.

The companies that made and sold DDT did not want people to find out these facts. They said that Rachel did not know what she was talking about.

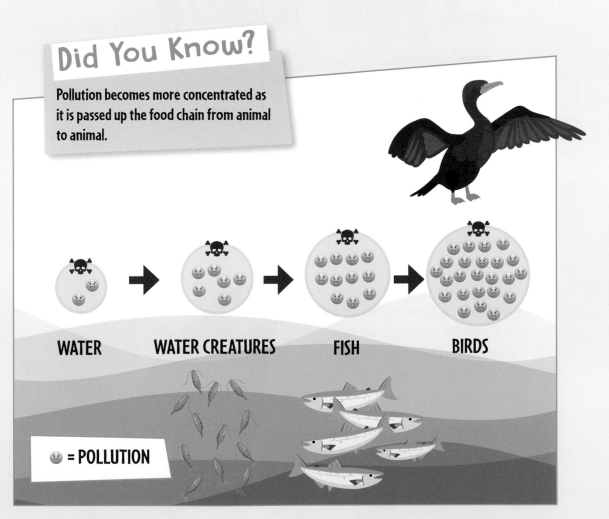

Did You Know?

Pollution becomes more concentrated as it is passed up the food chain from animal to animal.

WATER WATER CREATURES FISH BIRDS

😟 = POLLUTION

Rachel inspired many people to protect the environment.

By now, Rachel had found out that she was very sick, but she kept making her case. She went on TV to argue that the government needed to make new laws to protect the environment.

The US president at the time, John F. Kennedy, asked a group of experts to investigate Rachel's claims. The experts agreed with Rachel.

Rachel died on April 14, 1964, but her influence lived on. More and more people understood how fragile the natural world is. In 1970, the government set up the Environmental Protection Agency.

Readers of *Silent Spring* were upset by the idea of a world without birdsong.

In 1972, DDT was banned in the United States. It was replaced by less harmful pesticides.

Rachel's books also inspired ordinary people to help protect the natural world. People started environmental groups such as Greenpeace.

The environmental movement today includes millions of people around the world. **They are directly inspired by Rachel's work.**

In 2018, Swedish schoolgirl Greta Thunberg began "School Strike for Climate," a global campaign against climate change. ➡️

What Would You Do?

Rachel was very brave. She spoke out against a lot of people who tried to keep her quiet.

How could you keep yourself going in the face of opposition?

A big threat facing the environment today is climate change.

Would you go on a march or join a school strike against climate change?

If so, why?   **And if not, why not?**

At Work with Rachel Carson

Rachel worked in her study at home.

Writing *Silent Spring* brought together Rachel's two passions: writing and science! Discover more about how she created her famous book.

Typewriter

Rachel had the first idea for the book when she read that scientists were worried about the use of chemicals in farming. She began to gather facts about pesticides. Then the *New Yorker* magazine asked her to write an article about the pesticide DDT.

Rachel spent a lot of her time reading and making notes in medical libraries. She read about people who had become sick. She met experts who studied the causes of disease.

After all her research, Rachel became convinced that DDT was making people sick. She decided to expand her article into a longer, more detailed book.

Rachel knew her ideas would be **controversial**. Many people did not agree with her. She gathered as much evidence as possible and spent days checking her facts. She had to make sure her argument was solid.

When her research was complete, Rachel wrote *Silent Spring* on a typewriter in her study at her home in Silver Spring, Maryland. Her study had mirrored shelves to display her collection of seashells. The shells reminded her of the time she had spent studying the sea.

Rachel at work

Places of work: home study, National Library of Medicine, tidal pools

Daily activities: writing letters, making telephone calls, reading reports, writing articles

Main equipment: typewriter, microscope, telephone

Telephone   Microscope

Jane Goodall

SUPER SHERo OF SCIENCE

datafile

Born: 1934

Place of birth: United Kingdom

Field: Primatology

Super SHEro for: Showing people how to understand chimpanzees and the importance of preserving their **habitat**

Jane Goodall is a British scientist who studies **apes** and monkeys. She became famous for learning that chimpanzees are more like humans than anyone thought.

Jane was brought up by the English seaside. When she was a baby, her dad gave her a stuffed animal chimp instead of a teddy bear. The toy chimp was named Jubilee and Jane still had him when she was an adult. Growing up, Jane loved animals. She dreamed of working with animals in Africa.

In 1957, Jane's dream came true when she traveled to Kenya. There she became assistant to the famous **primatologist** Louis Leakey. Louis believed that the behavior of apes could teach us more about humans. He wanted Jane to observe chimpanzees. Jane studied animal behavior before she began her task.

Leakey asked Jane to study chimpanzees in the Gombe Stream National Park. In 1960, Jane traveled to the park in Tanzania to start work with local people. She would be living in the wild. At the time, women rarely traveled alone. Jane's mom went with her for safety.

Louis Leakey and his wife, Mary, found many fossils of early humans in Africa.

When Jane and her local helpers went into the jungle each day, the troop of chimps usually disappeared. Jane thought they were scared of people. After three months, she began to go alone to watch the chimps.

Things started to change. The chimps began to act more normally. One day, Jane saw a chimp trimming a stick to dig termites out of the ground. In the past, it had been thought that humans were the only animals that made tools. Jane's observation showed that belief was wrong.

Chimps push sticks into termite mounds to catch the insects. ➤

What's Your Story?

?

Jane was one of three women Louis Leakey asked to study primates. The three were nicknamed the Trimates. Jane studied chimps, Dian Fossey studied gorillas, and Birute Galdikas studied orangutans.

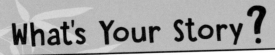

Have you ever studied or written a report on an animal?

If so, which animal did you pick?

Jane sat very still so she could get close to the chimps.

Over the next two years, Jane changed how people saw chimps. It had been thought that chimps were vegetarians, for example. Jane learned that they also ate meat. Jane wrote a book about her findings and became famous. In 1977, she set up the Jane Goodall Institute to protect the habitats of chimps and other wild animals.

Did You Know?

A chimp skull and a human skull are quite similar. Chimps and humans shared a common relative over 6 million years ago.

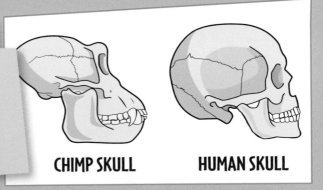

CHIMP SKULL   HUMAN SKULL

A chimp with her baby

During the twentieth century, the number of chimps in Africa fell by two-thirds, from around one million to fewer than 340,000. This was largely because people were cutting down forests for farmland. Jane wanted to convince locals to protect the chimps.

Forests were being cut down in Africa at an alarming rate, but the same thing was happening in many places in the world. A global problem required a global solution. Jane believed that saving **endangered** animals was best achieved by saving the whole planet.

Trees in Africa are being cut down at a rate about twice as fast as the global average.

Jane campaigned with other famous environmentalists, such as Prince Harry.

In 1991, Jane started the global Roots & Shoots movement with young people who were worried about the natural world. Jane wanted to show global leaders how local people could play a key role in protecting animals that lived near them.

Jane became a campaigner who spent her time writing and giving speeches about protecting the natural world. **She wanted to make Earth a better place for every living thing.**

What Would You Do?

Jane is most famous for her work studying chimpanzees. Chimpanzee numbers were falling in Africa. Around the world, many species are facing extinction.

What could you do to save a species from disappearing?

Jane became so friendly with the chimps that she could even touch them.

The way Jane studied chimps was new. Nobody had tried it before. Learn how she did it.

Camera

Jane was twenty-six when she first traveled to Gombe with her mom. Her mother stayed in camp while Jane went to study the chimpanzees. The camp was a tent, with snakes and scorpions crawling around. The kitchen was a firepit with a simple grass roof supported overhead on four poles.

As the chimps got used to Jane, they stopped running away. By keeping very still and wearing khaki-colored clothes, Jane blended into her surroundings. She spent many hours watching and noting the chimps' behavior. She was very brave. Chimps can be violent if they feel scared.

Jane gave the chimps names. Other primatologists usually gave animals numbers, but Jane was interested in the chimps' personalities. An adult male she named David Greybeard was the first chimp to approach and touch her. Jane's patience paid off when the other chimps also began to interact with her. They treated her as one of their community. They played with her and even allowed her to join in their grooming.

SUPER SHERO OF SCIENCE

Jane at work

Primary role: research

Places of work: Gombe Stream National Park, Tanzania

Daily activities: Watching the chimps, writing up her observations

Main equipment: Binoculars, camera, notepad and pen, typewriter

Typewriter

Binoculars

Emmanuelle Charpentier and Jennifer Doudna

SUPER SHEroes OF SCIENCE

datafile

Emmanuelle Charpentier (left)
Born: 1968

Place of birth: France

Field: Microbiology

Jennifer Doudna (right)
Born: 1964

Place of birth: United States

Field: Microbiology

Super SHEroes for:
Developing a way to prevent serious diseases

Emmanuelle Charpentier and Jennifer Doudna are **microbiologists**. They became famous for developing a way to prevent serious diseases.

Emmanuelle grew up near Paris, France, where she dreamed of making advances in medicine. She studied life sciences before joining the famous Pasteur Institute in Paris, where she studied **bacteria**. Emmanuelle did further research in the United States and Europe. Then she started studying **RNA**, a complex chemical compound that helps build cells inside living things and **viruses**.

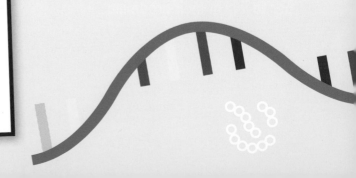

Jennifer was fascinated by the natural life of Hawaii.

At a conference in Puerto Rico in 2011, Emmanuelle met Jennifer Doudna. Jennifer was a biologist at the University of California. She grew up in Hawaii. As a kid, stories of medical advances inspired her, and she decided to devote her life to scientific research. Like Emmanuelle, Jennifer had studied RNA. The two women decided to work together to fight disease.

Did You Know?

RNA and DNA are not the same, though both perform very important functions in the cell! DNA is the molecule that codes life. It is the chemical material carried by genes, one of the parts that make up chromosomes (see page 9). Genes can be taken from one living thing and added to another living thing. This is called genetic engineering.

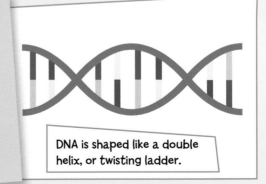

DNA is shaped like a double helix, or twisting ladder.

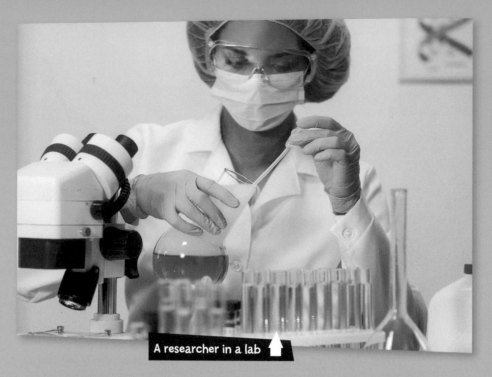

A researcher in a lab

Emmanuelle found a new type of RNA in bacteria. This RNA was special because it helped bacteria protect themselves from viruses. The RNA was able to guide a **protein** to cut up the DNA of the virus inside the bacteria. Cutting the DNA of the virus stopped the virus from spreading.

There are many different species, or types, of bacteria. They are tiny living things, which can be attacked by viruses, just as we can.

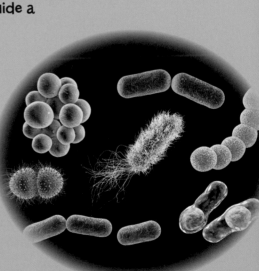

Emmanuelle and Jennifer figured out how to use this special type of RNA to guide a protein to make very precise cuts in the DNA of any living thing. It is as if they had created a pair of tiny scissors that can cut specific parts of DNA. Their discovery is now part of a tool known as CRISPR. CRISPR revolutionized genetic engineering. It makes it possible to change the DNA of plants or animals by cutting out specific parts of DNA that may cause diseases.

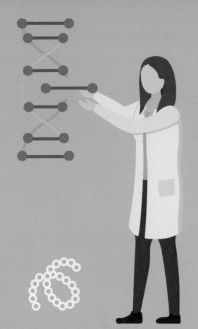

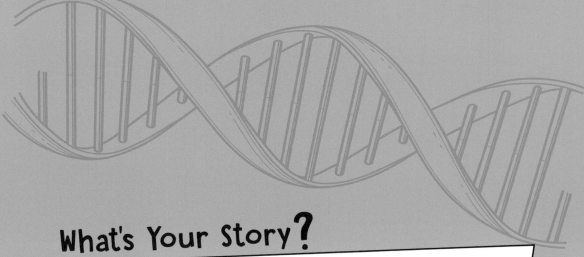

What's Your Story?

At high school in Hawaii, Jennifer was inspired by a chemistry teacher named Jeanette Wong. Jennifer later said of Jeanette, "She showed me that science is about answering questions, not memorizing facts."

Which teacher or subject has inspired you in school?

In 2020, Emmanuelle and Jennifer won the Nobel Prize in Chemistry for their breakthrough. It was the first time a female team had won the award.

Emmanuelle and Jennifer pose with a poster of DNA.

Winning the Nobel Prize made Emmanuelle and Jennifer two of the most famous scientists on the planet. Since then, they have both continued their own research into ways to use genetic engineering to improve health. Jennifer works at the University of Berkeley, California, while Emmanuelle works at a famous research organization, the Max Planck Institute in Berlin.

CRISPR is also used to change crops so they can resist insects.

Today CRISPR is used in many ways. It is used to prevent mosquitoes from spreading the disease malaria. It also stops some genetic diseases being passed on from parents to their children. **Emmanuelle and Jennifer grew up wanting to help cure diseases—and they succeeded!**

What Would You Do?

Genetic engineering is used to make medicines and cure sickness. It is also used to improve crops so there is more food for people to eat.

Do you think people should artificially change natural things?

What ways would you improve crops?

Investigating **Nature** DISEASES

HiLdegard of Bingen

Hildegard of Bingen
(Germany, 1098-1179)

Hildegard was a nun in Germany in the twelfth century. Her duties included looking after the sick, and she became one of the first women to write a catalog of how plants and minerals could be used to cure diseases.

Hildegard believed the human body should mirror the world. In that way, she was one of the first people to suggest that there was a close link between individuals and the health of the whole planet. That belief is now the foundation of the modern environmental movement.

Mary Anning

Mary Anning was born in southwest England. She helped her father find ancient animal fossils from nearby cliffs to sell in his store. Mary also collected fossils to sell herself. When Mary was just twelve, she and her brother found the fossilized skeleton of an animal no one had ever seen before. It was named an ichthyosaur, or fish-lizard.

Later Mary discovered the first plesiosaur, a large marine mammal. She also found a pterosaur, which was a flying reptile. Some scientists did not believe Mary's fossils were real at first. But her discoveries went on to change our understanding of how life on planet Earth has changed over time.

Mary Anning
(United Kingdom, 1799-1847)

Mary found the complete fossilized skeleton of a plesiosaur.

Nettie Stevens

Nettie Stevens was an early expert in genetics at Bryn Mawr College, Pennsylvania. Nettie studied mealworms and discovered the pair of chromosomes that influenced whether they would be male or female. The sex of many animals is influenced by a similar pair of chromosomes, known as X and Y.

Nettie Stevens
(United States, 1861-1912)

Roger Arliner Young
(United States, 1899-1964)

Roger Arliner Young

Investigating
Nature
MARINE ANIMALS

Roger Arliner Young became the first Black woman in the United States to earn a doctorate in zoology and to publish a paper in the important journal *Science*. Roger explored the effects of **radiation** on marine animals.

Ynes Mexia

Mexican American botanist Ynes Mexia was one of the most successful plant collectors of her time. Born in Washington, DC, she spent most of her life in Mexico before moving to San Francisco, where she joined campaigns to save the redwood forests of California.

When she was fifty-one years old, Ynes decided to study botany at the University of Berkeley, California. On her first plant-collecting trip to Mexico, she collected 1,500 species. Ynes began a thirteen-year career traveling through the Americas, often alone. She collected more than 145,000 plant specimens, including more than 500 plants that had not been recorded before.

Ynes Mexia
(United States, 1870-1938)

Rosalind Franklin

Investigating **Nature** DNA

The English scientist Rosalind Franklin used X-rays to study chemical molecules. Among the subjects she studied were coal, graphite (the "lead" in pencils), and viruses.

Her most famous work concerned the structure of DNA. Rosalind was the person who realized that one photograph revealed clues that DNA is a double helix. This insight allowed scientists to finally understand DNA's structure. This was key in understanding how DNA works.

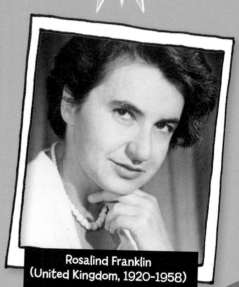

Rosalind Franklin (United Kingdom, 1920-1958)

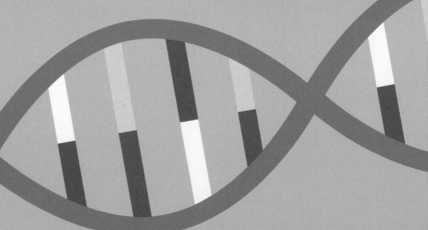

Lynn Margulis

Lynn Margulis was an American biologist who first suggested that complex cells like the ones in our bodies were created from bacteria. She argued that groups of bacteria came together to work as a team. Her theory was rejected but was later accepted. She also helped develop a view of Earth called the Gaia Hypothesis. This suggests that the planet keeps its conditions just right for life.

Lynn Margulis
(United States, 1938–2011)

Sylvia Earle

Sylvia Earle is one of the most high-profile scientists in the world. She is a marine biologist. She became the first female director of the US National Ocean and Atmospheric Administration (NOAA), responsible for studying the oceans and the air. She speaks widely about the importance of looking after our planet, working with magazines such as *Time* and *National Geographic* to spread knowledge.

Sylvia Earle
(United States, born 1935)

TimeLine

Here are some highlights in the history of investigating nature.

Janaki Ammal becomes director of India's Central Botanical Laboratory.

Jane Goodall begins fifteen years of studying chimpanzees at Gombe Stream National Park in Tanzania.

Ynes Mexia begins her first plant-collecting trip to Mexico.

Researchers confirm the double helix structure of DNA.

| 1905 | 1925 | 1940 | 1947 | 1952 | 1953 | 1960 | 1962 |

Nettie Stevens discovers the role of chromosomes in determining sex.

Roger Arliner Young is the first Black woman to achieve a doctorate in zoology.

Rachel Carson publishes *Silent Spring*, explaining the harm pesticides do to the environment.

Rosalind Franklin realizes that an X-ray image contains clues to the structure of DNA.

Lynn Margulis publishes her theory about the evolution of animal and plant cells from bacteria.

The US government passes the Endangered Species Act to protect wildlife.

Sylvia Earle becomes the first female Chief Scientist at the National Ocean and Atmospheric Administration (NOAA).

Emmanuelle Charpentier and Jennifer Doudna jointly win the Nobel Prize for Chemistry.

| 1970 | 1972 | 1973 | 1977 | 1990 | 2011 | 2020 |

DDT is banned in the United States.

Jane Goodall sets up the Jane Goodall Institute to preserve natural environments.

Emmanuelle Charpentier and Jennifer Doudna meet at a conference and begin to work together.

41

1. Janaki Ammal
Coimbatore, Tamil Nadu, India
Janaki worked at this sugarcane breeding station in the early 1930s.

2. Mary Anning
Dorset, England
Mary hunted for fossils in the cliffs near her home. The area is now known as the Jurassic Coast for its many fossils.

3. Rachel Carson
Silver Spring, Maryland
Rachel wrote *Silent Spring* at her new home in Silver Spring, Maryland, north of Washington, DC.

4. Emmanuelle Charpentier
Berlin, Germany
Emmanuelle founded a laboratory in Berlin in 2018 to study causes of disease.

5. Jennifer Doudna
Berkeley, California
Jennifer founded an institute to study genetics at the University of California at Berkeley.

6. Sylvia Earle
Virgin Islands
In 1970, Sylvia led four female scientists in an experiment in which they lived in a special home built on the seabed.

7. Rosalind Franklin
London, England
Rosalind worked at University College in London, but her discoveries benefited many scientists working elsewhere.

North America

Atlantic Ocean

Pacific Ocean

South America

N

8. Jane Goodall

Gombe National Park, Tanzania
Jane's work at Gombe Stream National Park is continued by a research center.

10. Lynn Margulis

Boston, Massachusetts
Lynn was a junior professor at Boston University. She found it hard to get promoted because her ideas were so unusual.

11. Ynes Mexia

Puerto Vallarta, Jalisco, Mexico
Ynes collected the flowering plant Mexianthus, which was named for her, near Puerto Vallarta.

12. Nettie Stevens

Washington, DC
Nettie worked at the Carnegie Institute of Washington when she published her breakthrough findings about chromosomes.

9. Hildegard of Bingen

Bingen am Rhein, Germany
Hildegard founded a convent at Rupertsberg in 1150, where she spent fifteen years studying nature, music, and religion.

13. Roger Arliner Young

Woods Hole, Massachusetts
Roger did marine research at the Oceanographic Institution at Woods Hole on the New England coast.

Words of Wisdom

Read the inspirational words of these
Super SHEroes of Science and remember:
You can become a Super SHEro, too!

Jane Goodall

❝ You cannot get through a single day without having an impact on the world around you. What you do makes a difference, and you have to decide what kind of difference you want to make. **❞**

❝ Glance at the sun. See the moon and the stars. Gaze at the beauty of the Earth's greenings. Now, think. **❞**
Hildegard of Bingen

Rachel Carson

❝ The aim of science is to discover and illuminate truth. **❞**

Jennifer Doudna

❝ The more we know, the more we realize there is to know. **❞**

Emmanuelle Charpentier

66 It's very important to provide a very positive message for the girls and the young women who wish to start science, continue in science, and to really provide a clear message that it is possible to achieve ultimate recognition, even if you are female. 99

66 Science and everyday life cannot and should not be separated. 99
Rosalind Franklin

Janaki Ammal

66 I am a born wanderer. There is a great restlessness in me. 99

66 The best scientists and explorers have the attributes of kids! They ask questions and have a sense of wonder. They have curiosity. 'Who, what, where, why, when, and how!' They never stop asking questions, and I never stop asking questions, just like a five-year-old. 99
Sylvia Earle

Glossary

apes (apes) large animals related to monkeys and humans

bacteria (bak-**teer**-ee-uh) tiny one-celled organisms

biodiversity (*bye*-oh-duh-**vur**-si-tee) the variety of plants and animals living in an area

biology (bye-**ah**-luh-jee) the study of living things

botany (**bah**-tuh-nee) the scientific study of plant life

chromosomes (**kroh**-muh-*sohmz*) structures inside a cell nucleus that carry genes

controversial (*kahn*-truh-**vur**-shuhl) causing a great deal of disagreement

discrimination (dis-*krim*-i-**nay**-shuhn) unfair treatment of others based on differences in things such as gender or race

DNA the molecule that carries genes inside the nucleus of cells. DNA is short for deoxyribonucleic acid.

endangered (en-**dayn**-jurd) in danger of becoming extinct

environment (en-**vye**-ruhn-muhnt) the natural surroundings of living things

extinction (ik-**stingk**-shun) the permanent disappearance of a species

fossils (**fah**-suhlz) traces of ancient life preserved as rocks

genes (jeenz) chemical signals from parents that determine how children grow

habitat (**hab**-i-*tat*) the place where a plant or animal is usually found

laboratory (**lab**-ruh-*tor*-ee) a room or building with special equipment for scientific experiments

microbiologists (*mye*-kroh-bye-**ah**-luh-jists) scientists who study tiny organisms, such as bacteria

pesticide (**pes**-ti-*side*) a chemical used to kill pests, such as insects

primates (**prye**-matz) the group of mammals that includes monkeys, apes, and humans

primatologist (*prye*-muh-**tol**-uh-jist) someone who studies primates

protein (**proh**-teen) a chemical that creates tissue in living things

radiation (ray-dee-**ay**-shuhn) atomic particles sent out by a radioactive substance

RNA The complex molecule produced by living cells and viruses that manufactures the protein in a cell. RNA is short for ribonucleic acid.

species (**spee**-sheez) a group of related animals or plants that can breed together

viruses (**vye**-ruhs-ez) single-celled particles capable of causing disease

Index

Page numbers in **bold** refer to illustrations

Further Reading

Ford, Michael. *Rosalind Franklin: DNA Pioneer* (A Life Story). New York: Scholastic, 2020.

Ignotofsky, Rachel. *Women in Science: 50 Fearless Pioneers Who Changed the World*. New York: Crown Books for Young Readers, 2021.

Rooney, Anne. *Rachel Carson* (Women in Science). New York: Scholastic, 2019.

Taylor-Butler, Christine. *Genetics* (True Books). New York: Scholastic, 2016.

Woolf, Alex. *Jane Goodall* (Women in Science). New York: Scholastic, 2020.

About the Author

Anita Dalal grew up in an Anglo-Indian family in northern England. She studied for her PhD in London and traveled widely around the world, including many visits with her family in India, before settling in London with her own family. She has written many books for children, often about history and geography. She loved learning new facts about some of her scientific heroines for this book—and discovering other Super SHEroes of Science for the first time! When she's not in the library or at her desk working, she spends her time gardening, walking Monty the golden Labrador, and watching her son play sports. She loves swimming outdoors—even when it's freezing!

About the Consultant

Isabel Thomas is a science communicator and American Association for the Advancement of Science award-winning author. She has degrees in Human Sciences from the University of Oxford and in Education Research from the University of Cambridge, where her academic research focused on addressing inequalities in aspiration and access to science education and careers.